Recordir

How I Made $100k A Year From Home!

By John Rogers

RecordingStudioSecrets.com

Copyright 2019

TABLE OF CONTENTS

TABLE OF CONTENTS

Who This Book Is For

This book is for someone who is either just starting an online recording studio or already has one, and would like to know *how I* increased my income to over $100k a year.

Audio mixing and/or mastering is a highly rewarding career. You're helping people fulfill a life long dream. You make their music sound great, and most are highly appreciative of your efforts. **And you get paid for this too!**

It's not like the 9-5 job where you're over worked, underpaid, and your income is capped. Not to mention unappreciated.

As an audio engineer, you are your own boss. You set *your own* schedule. This high flexibility allows to work on other projects, or even another job if you choose to do so. It's also extra free time to enjoy life!

The sky's the limit when it comes to your income! This being a service business, there are only so many hours in a week. But you're not capped. $150k plus a year is possible if you build your business and expand it to videos, affiliate programs, etc. Unlike many 9-5 jobs that are a dead end with no light at the end of the tunnel.

70% of America either hates their career or don't have one. **Do something you love!** Audio engineering is fun and easy work.

Also like I mentioned earlier, you're appreciated for your work too! It's an amazing feeling when you do a great job for a customer and they thank you multiple times for it.

I wrote this entire book in simple plain English (layman's terms). I eliminated all the words you never heard of and hi-tech jargon, so anyone at any level can understand and learn from this book.

For a very small investment, let me show you everything I've learned over the past 19 years about building a successful online recording studio.

What You Will Learn From This Book

In this book I explain everything I did to build my online recording studio business, so that it brought in over $100k a year.

This is what "I" did, and it worked for me. I also mention a few things that didn't work (so you can avoid them).

Before I get into what I cover in this book, I would like to mention it's not a get rich quick book.

I'll tell you right now, making $100k a year as an online audio engineer is a business/client building process.

My first *month* online I made only $150. My second *month* I made $250. I made $10,000 my first *year,* and $45,000 my second *year.* It wasn't until my third year that I started making $100k plus. But I am VERY happy I stuck with it.

In this book, I explain:

- My formula for a profitable online studio
- The marketing I used to promote my studio
- Working with difficult customers
- How to beat out the competition with your free demos
- Creating your website
- And more!

About The Author

Hello, my name is John Rogers. I'm a professional sound engineer and have been mixing and mastering at my Las Vegas studio http://JRmastering.com, since 1999. **I've worked with over 7,500 highly satisfied customers and mastered over 40,000 songs in every genre and style imaginable.**

I've worked with several Grammy nominees and award winners (Bowling for Soup, Sir Charles Jones, Mary J Blige, Dionne Warwick, Ryan Saranich). I've also mastered many billboard top 10 songs in Europe (Smiley, Nyls, Andra, Miss Mary), movie soundtracks, videos that have appeared on MTV, and dance/EDM music that has been played in dance clubs all around the world.

After receiving *thousands* of highly favorable email comments from my clients, most not believing what I achieved with their music, I realized I have great audio mastering skills. And in conjunction with great business principles, I was able to build a highly successful online business. **Let me show you exactly how I did it!**

Testimonials

Here are a handful of testimonials from the over 7,500 clients I've worked with since 1999. **I want you to know you'll be learning from an audio engineer that not only achieves *amazing* mastering results, but also displays a high-level of professionalism, patience, and speed.** I do everything I can to get my clients' music sounding the very best it can! And treat each project as if it were my own. http://JRmastering.com

That is very kind of you to give me such detailed notes on ways I can improve future mixes and recordings.... I've been reading up on your mixing tips articles, and they are very informative, but having something that's personalized feedback on my mixes is beyond fantastic! I really want to thank you, John, again for everything, all the tips, all your time and work, you've got loyal clients here, I will certainly continue to always bring my business your way... **Aaron F.**

Every project I work on always goes to John! He has an awesome way of turning your track into something really great! I always suggest him to other producers. I will continue to use him on ALL my tracks, and I would recommend him for all of your projects! **Jake W.**

I don't now how you do it, but you are amazing! You are so dead on with your instincts and skills. I'm gonna drop $36 into your PayPal account. Keep the extra $30 as a tip. Go have a beer on me. An EXPENSIVE one! Wow, you have just blown me away with your work. I'm coming to you every single time, man. You are the tops. Give me a call anytime you need anything, and if I can help, I will. And when we gear up for our next CD, I'll give you a shout. Thanks again, man. You're just awesome. **Felix**

SETTING UP YOUR LISTENING ENVIRONMENT

Note – This section is also included in my other books. **It's so critical to your success that I included it in this book**, *just incase you don't buy any of my other books.*

An audio engineers job starts with your listening environment. **If it isn't giving you a *true* sound, you'll be lost.**

Room Size

Technically, you can properly mix or master in any room size. But, I believe a *smaller* room is better than a very large one for someone who's just starting out. And when I say *smaller* I mean closer to 12'x15' than to 20'x30'. I've mixed and mastered songs for a number of years in a 20'x30' room. It took me a few days to get used to it, but after that I could do it.

The obvious problem with a big room is it's a very open space. If you don't have a good acoustic setup, the room will add reverb to every song.

You have to compensate for this on every song you mix or master, because the extra reverb you hear isn't really in the music. It's coming from the room.

In a smaller room, even with no acoustic treatment, your mixes and masters will all sound more true. They won't be discolored from bouncing around a big room.

Speaker Choices

I've used dozens of different brands of speakers in my career and I do like a few better than others. But, this article deals more with types and sizes of speakers, not with the brand choices. For *my* free brand choices – **HomeStudioGearSecrets.com**

The main mixing and mastering speakers I currently use are Dynaudio 100w powered studio monitors with 6" woofers and 1.1" tweeters. They have nice EQ adjustment options on the back and I know these speakers very well. If you get speakers that are a little larger, you'll get better LOW-end out of them, but I'm happy with the size I use.

The most important part of your speaker setup (that a lot of newbies don't know about) is having a sub-woofer on the floor between your main studio monitors. If you're using 4-6" monitor speakers, it's *impossible* to correctly mix or master any music content under 150hz without having a sub-woofer. 4-6" studio monitors will not play the low 60hz sub-bass *AT ALL*, and they're weak at best in the 100hz area.

Speaker Placement

Before I tell you the setup I like best, after *many* years of experimentation, I'd like to first tell you the setup I personally don't like (even though *a lot* of sound engineers do this). Two studio monitors, five feet apart, on a desk *two feet away from their face.* And NO sub-woofer! I think they call this "near field" monitoring.

But at some point during the audio mastering process, you *must* crank the music up very loud to set your final compression and to hear how it translates at high volume levels. You can't do this if your speakers are right next to your ears! At least I can't.

Maybe this is why the songs I get in for re-mastering badly break up when cranked up loud, and the bass is totally washed out. They were originally mastered at very low levels without a sub-woofer, and not optimized for loud playback.

I also find it hard determining the overall depth and stereo width in music when the speakers are two feet in front of me. Which makes sense. Its like watching a 50" TV. I want it to be far enough away so I can take the whole picture in. No one puts a 50" TV on a table right in front of them, yet this is done with speakers.

My Personal Speaker Placement

First off, I use speaker stands for my studio monitors, and the speakers stand 3.5 feet off the ground. I have the stands roughly 7 feet apart, and the speakers are about 6-7 feet away from my face. The sub-woofer is on the floor, centered between the two speaker stands.

Note - **Do not put the back of the speakers right up against a wall.** Have at least 10 inches between the back of your speakers and the wall, or the sound will be altered.

I've found this setup is close enough where I can here all the details in the music, wide enough so I get a full representation of the stereo field, and the speakers are far away enough so I can crank the music up to 105dbs to make sure it sounds right for loud playback, without blasting myself in the face.

Learning And Calibrating Your Speakers

When I first start out with NEW speakers (though I never change them now), I listen to my favorite hit songs in every genre and style. Songs that I know from my years of experience have X amount of bass, X amount of brightness, etc. **I know how these songs are "supposed" to sound.**

Most good speakers have EQ adjustment switches on them, and the sub-woofer has a volume control on it. After several listens, I'll slightly adjust the EQ on the monitor speakers and the bass amount on the sub-woofer so that my favorite reference songs sound "true" to me. I'm making my speakers sound true to life, not exaggerated in any sonic area. **Once the songs playing through these speakers sound "true" to me, then anything I mix or master will be done correctly.**

How could speakers sound _untrue_ to me? An example, if I'm playing a few commercially hip hop songs and the bass sounds very weak on every song, the speakers I'm using are _untrue_ because I know _in reality_ the bass should be _much_ higher/louder in hip hop. I know the sub-woofer needs the bass volume adjusted and maybe the studio monitors do too. And I adjust them accordingly.

If I worked with these untrue speakers, I would improperly raise the bass on every song, thinking it was too low, when in reality the speakers aren't properly playing the bass.

It's easier when working with _true_ speakers because what you hear correctly represents the audio material you're working on.

Sound Proofing Your Room

Way too much is made out of room sound proofing. I've audio mastered songs to perfection in an untreated basement (when I started out), in huge and small treated pro studio rooms, and I've had several song that were on the radio in Europe, that ranked on the billboard charts, that were ALL mastered in a quiet small UNTREATED bedroom. No one can honestly say it can't be done, **I have the radio masters to prove it.**

You will have to listen to a few reference tracks using good speakers you know well, to learn your environment. And some client feedback is required. But after some practice, you can do it.

Now, If your listening space echoes or just sounds to wide, by all means deaden the sound. **Remember, your goal is to get a true sound in your room.** But, If your studio is a small carpeted room, **you don't necessarily _need_ foam or sound proofing on your walls.** You already have a quiet room. The important thing is to learn your listening environment, whatever it is.

Note - **If you feel you *have to* have some foam or acoustic treatment in your room, BUY IT!** Remember, you'll still have to learn how the room sounds after you install it. **Many don't get this part right and their work is very poor.**

Again, my point is you don't necessarily *need it* for audio mastering if your room doesn't reverberate or heavily color the audio. This is common sense. But, I see too many people online that won't start mixing and mastering until they can scrape up $1,000 for room treatment.

I've gotten in hundreds of remaster jobs that were originally mastered at studios with thousands of dollars worth of foam on their walls, and these masters were HORRENDOUS! A mash of distorted noise trainwreck! **The foam did a lot of good for them...**

PROTECTING YOUR HEARING

Note – This section is also included in my other books. ***It's so critical to your success that I included it in this book,*** *just incase you don't buy any of my other books.*

Millions of people suffer from tinnitus. A new study shows around 10% of the U.S. population suffers from it in some form, **but many have never even heard of it until they got it!** Unfortunately, I was one of those people. It can happen quickly and it lasts a lifetime...

As a sound engineer, your hearing is your most important asset. It's critical that you protect it for as long as possible. In this section, I will discuss the causes and prevention of tinnitus, and general safety practices that will help you keep your ears healthy.

What Is Tinnitus?

Tinnitus is the constant hearing of a sound when there is no sound present. Some describe it as a ringing sound, a hiss, or a high pitched tone. The sound is continual, and it varies from one tinnitus suffer to another.

How Is Tinnitus Caused?

Tinnitus is caused by either a single extremely loud sound or by loud sounds over a period of time. I know a military vet who got severe tinnitus from the sound of jets taking off in close proximity.

Another guy I know got it from a single bomb explosion that was right next to him. Listening to loud music at a concert or club, if you're in a band, if you play music loud on your iPod, or monitoring music very loud as a sound engineer; over a period of time *any* of these scenarios could cause tinnitus. If you cut grass for a living and don't wear earplugs, I would imagine that could eventually cause it too.

It can also be caused by prescription drugs in the benzodiazepine family or even by over the counter drugs like ibuprofen. I heard of a man who got severe tinnitus from MSG in Chinese food. The cook made a mistake and loaded it up heavy with MSG.

How Did I Get My Tinnitus And How Did It Sound?

I got tinnitus in 1999, working on one of my very first mastering projects the day I opened my studio, JR mastering. At that time, I needed to listen to the songs much longer than I do now because of my lack of experience, and I listened to them WAY too loud.

I was reviewing my final masters at a high volume level (105-110 dbs) for about 30 minutes non-stop. When I was finished I didn't really notice anything. But, when night time came I could hear a high-pitched tone. It sounded like a 40db test tone @ 5k. I could hear the tone in both ears, but my right ear was twice as bad as my left.

The first few days it was hard for me to sleep because I kept thinking about this sound. The sound was also very annoying when sitting outside in a quiet area.

Is There A Cure For Tinnitus?

No. There are many pills and snake oil products online, but I have never heard of a valid cure. But, experts say it gets better over time as long as you don't make it worse.

The first few months I suffered from tinnitus, I would say it was very annoying at night but not too bad during the day. It did not effect my sound engineering. After six months, it improved about 25%. After a year, it's roughly 50% better. Now, many years later, I would say I have maybe 20% of the original tinnitus I got in 1999 (an 80% improvement). Its pretty much gone because it was a mild case of tinnitus to begin with, and I took preventative measures so it wouldn't get worse.

Can You Mix And Master Music With Tinnitus?

Mine was not severe, so it did not hinder me at all. The noise I heard was a 40db loud test tone @ 5k. I started doing my initial mixing and mastering at around 85dbs, so the tinnitus tone was pretty much masked (drowned out). Its kind of like when someone records mic hiss. You can hear it when the music stops, but when the guitars are playing you can't hear it at all because the hiss is being masked.

Singer Phil Collins retired because of his tinnitus. Bono also has very severe tinnitus that greatly affects his everyday life. **If your tinnitus is very severe like those two, I'm sure your sound engineering skills would be *greatly* affected.**

How To Prevent Tinnitus In Everyday Life

Always use hearing protection (earplugs) when at a concert or a club playing loud music, when cutting grass, when using a blower or electric power tools, and for sure when shooting a gun. Any situation where a continuous 100db sound is present.

Also, don't listen to music over 100dbs for long periods of time. OSHA recommends no more than 1 hour @ 105dbs. **I would NEVER go more than 20 minutes straight at 105dbs, if that.** Also, be careful with ibuprofen and prescription drugs.

How Loud Is Too Loud When Mixing And Mastering?

Well, 105-110dbs for 30 minutes straight was too loud for me. I had tinnitus at the end of the 30-minute session! Everyone is different, so I don't want to give you specific sound ranges and upper limits. All I can tell you is what gave me tinnitus, and what's worked for me to improve my tinnitus 80% since 1999.

How To Protect Your Hearing As A Sound Engineer

THE GUINEA PIG EXPERIMENT

I read a study online where a scientist exposed guinea pigs to extremely loud music. The results were that the guinea pigs who listened to extremely loud music *continuously*, say for 30 minutes, had *severe* structural damage to their internal ears.

The guinea pigs who listened to the same extremely loud 30 minutes of music, *but* it was *not continuous* (roughly 2 minutes of music and then a 2 minute break), the damage to their internal ears was *FAR LESS* severe compared to the first group.

Now remember, both groups listened to music the same total time (30 minutes). But, *continuous* listening was far more damaging than *intermittent* listening.

The Rules I Follow During Music Mixing And Mastering

I initially mix and master at a lower level. I keep levels around 80-90dbs. I listen 10-15 minutes at these levels, then take a 5-minute break. I will do this for between 2-4 hours, then I take a full two-hour break.

When it comes time for the finalization (loud listening @ 105-110dbs) I NEVER go more than 2-3 minutes continuous and I pretty much split time. If I listen to loud music for 5 minutes, I take a 5 minute break before starting up again.

Above is what I've been doing since 1999 and it works for me. Maybe you can go 100dbs for 8 hours a day and never have a problem, but I'm not risking it. **105-110dbs for 30 minutes continuous ruined my ears pretty good, and I had to make sure they didn't get any worse.**

Tinnitus isn't fun. I might be going overboard a bit with my silence rests, but it's working for me. **Better safe than sorry with tinnitus because it lasts A LIFETIME!**

THE FORMULA FOR A PROFITABLE ONLINE STUDIO

When building my online business to earn $100k a year online, there wasn't *one* magic thing I did to make it happen, but rather *several* things in combination. In this chapter I will go over each one.

1. How I Got My FREE Traffic

Free Traffic is the result of your marketing efforts.

$500 in failed Google test ads was the only money I ever spent marketing my online studio. All my traffic is FREE!

"Traffic is by far the number one element of any successful business."

Yes, many factors are important, but without potential clients/customers, sales are *impossible* for any business.

And I say **"by far number one"** because the more traffic you have, the more mistakes you can cover up in other areas of your business and still be highly profitable. Also, you have more chances for a sale. **A *good* salesman with 1,000 hot leads will destroy an *amazing* salesman with 10 leads.**

THE POWER OF HEAVY TRAFFIC!

In the late 90s, I was a major part of the marketing team for a top online sportsbook. The guys who ran the company were great guys to me, but the business was run poorly in many areas.

The problems - their betting software was a little glitchy, misleading free bonuses pissed off customers, and very slow payouts (30 days or more) were common. **Some customer didn't get paid at all!** And this all lead to *many* terrible reviews, bad word of mouth, and of course the people who got stiffed never came back.

Ok, so you probably think this company went out of business rather quickly. Wrong! I would say they made roughly $1 million profit in their first year, and by the third year they were making **a million *a month*!** Their best year they made at least $30 million (maybe even $50 million) before things started to decline.

How could this company be so successful making this many mistakes?

Two reasons.

1. They were one of only five online sportsbook. "The only game in town" factor. Options were limited if you wanted to wager online.

2. The biggest reason was huge traffic. The first year they were getting 5,000 visitors a day to the website, and 1,000 clients a week *deposited cash.*

And you never knew what each person would deposit. They had a Wisconsin cheese mogul who **lost $100,000 a month** for years. I didn't say *wagered* $100,000 a month. *He LOST $100,000 a month.* I wish I could have booked his action! Ha! The dude never won.

Note – The guy wagered with this company for many years because *he was never stiffed out of his winnings.* There were no winnings to stiff him out of.

This sportbook didn't care about repeat visitors. If they cheated a few people here and there, or got a few bad reviews, they just signed up a ton of new clients the next month. At one point it was 10,000 a month. New money was constant. **You can see in this scenario how traffic covers up mistakes**.

Note – I *do not* condone poorly running your business or scamming and then turning profit with huge traffic numbers. I was just giving an example of how huge traffic (new clients) can cover up other business mistakes.

Even at the peak of my online studio business, I was making good money but I could not afford to make critical mistakes and still sustain any success. **I had to excel in every area.**

Now in late 2019, 40% of my business is from repeat customers, studios and labels. I want you to realize that this doesn't happen if a business is run poorly.

Doing things right now has future benefits.

HOW DID I GET MY FREE TRAFFIC?

First, I had to create a website. I used Joomla as my CMS, and **http://BestMusicHosting.com** (In Motion) has been my hosting company for all of my websites since 2009. I will probably never leave this company.

I used a number of different websites to generate traffic to my site. All FREE! *Google Search was #1* for me, but I will go through all of them.

A. Google Search (60%)

(more than half my traffic came from Google search)

Note - The secret to a high ranking in Google search changes every 6-12 months.

Now in mid-2019, their focus is on -
Name branding, backlinks/social media mentions, and great content. Your website needs to be solid in these areas if you want to rank high in the Google search results.

<u>Name Branding –</u>
When it comes to your website's homepage, **Google now focuses more on *brand names* than they do on *keywords*.** They want to know which *companies* are the best in each industry, and their search result try to rank them in that order.

Note - **Keywords on your home page are still important.** They help Google determine *what* your company/brand name is all about.

Backlinks/Social Media Mentions –

Back in the day, you linked your backlinks to *keywords* to try and rank for that *keyword*. Website search results showed mostly *keywords* in the titles. Now, Google wants *company names* to appear in the titles.

When you type in "mastering service" Google wants titles like -

JR Mastering Services

NOT -

Mastering Service | Music Mastering | Audio Mastering

To improve your search rank, you want most of your backlinks to be linked to your *brand name (company name)*. And, these backlinks should be on websites *related to your industry* and in the same language as your site.

So, backlinks on Russian and Chinese websites are now GREATLY devalued....

Also, social media mentions is now a ranking factor (according to Google).

I have personally noticed this to be a factor for tough keywords.

Example - Someone used my studio and tweets, "JR mastering is great!" A Facebook post says, "Your company is amazing."

Google somehow factors these positive comments into your ranking. Note – They also factor in "Your company sucks" too.

Google's logic is if there are thousands of people mentioning a website and saying great things about it, the website is a popular great company. And it should rank higher in the search. Is Google right?

Well, not if the company hired a bunch of people from India to make fake social media posts. Ha!

Great Content -
(Google says this is also a ranking factor)

This is self explanatory, but it's hard to imagine how the Google search software can read the content on a website and tell if it's great or not.

How long someone stays on your page is how I think they do it. If every visitor to your site is back on Google search after 10 seconds, Google can assume your site isn't that good or it's not relevant to the search results. If they stay on your site for a long time, that's a good thing.

If you do a few mixing/mastering keyword searches, you will find many websites in the low top 10 that have only a few pages on them. What I'm saying is 5-10 page websites are beating out 200 page websites. **So, it looks like content *volume* isn't that important.**

Though Google says "great content" is a factor, I don't feel it's a very strong one.

GOOGLE AD TIPS

I wanted to throw this in, just in case you want to try Google paid keyword search ads.

I spent hundreds of thousands of dollars in Google search ads in the early 2000's for other businesses and did *extremely* well, but haven't done much with my online studio business.

I purchase $500 in Google pay per click test ads. I spent $500 @ $1.50 a click and got in $400. That's a loss!

At roughly $1.50 per click at the time of this writing, most companies will not show a profit at this price in the online recording studio market.

Proof of this is the $1.50 bid has been stuck there for a couple years. There's no bidding. **Profitable click bids rise. Once they stop, there's no money to be made with them any more.**

When I started working with the sportsbook (mentioned in this book) it cost only 0.50 a click, and then $1, for top keywords. A year later it was $10 a click. At its peak, $35 a click!

If there was no profit at say $5 a click, there would have been no bidding. I would guess $25 a click maxed out any decent profits.

IMPORTANT - When it comes to clicks on your keywords, you have to consider at least 25% of the clicks are *competitors* and another 25% are *fakes* (90% fakes if you don't setup your account properly).

That means only 50% of your clicks are true potential customers. This has to be factored in.

If you are going to give Google search ads a try, KNOW THIS!

1. I don't use the mobile network.

I've found it's not worth it because potential clients don't have their music on their phones and can't upload a song for a free demo. **I found it to be window shopping with no one returning.**

2. DO NOT use the Google partner network. Use Google search only.

The Google partner network is comprised of *affiliate sites* that show your ads for a cut of the click money. It's in their best interest to click on your ads because they make money. **And they do it!**

True story. I had $150 in free promo Google money. I placed some recording studio keyword ads up and **forgot** to *turn off* **mobile** and **partner network**. I hit the button and started the campaign.

IN 15 MINUTES THE ENTIRE $150 (100 CLICKS) WAS GONE! WHAT!

Great, 100 visitors in 15 minutes, I'm going to be rich! WRONG!

I looked at my clicky stats and 95 of the 100 clicks were from partner sites on a mobile phone. That's not necessarily a bad thing. But the fact that all **95 supposed visitors were on the website for under 10 seconds before leaving MEANS THE TRAFFIC WAS ALL FAKE.**

I know my clicks were fake because they all left the site in under 10 seconds. My legit visitors averages 2-4 minutes each. At least a minute shows a probable legit visitor. But under 10 seconds?

I don't know why Google even does this. It's basically a legal scam.

Some companies don't know anything about Google search ads, put $10,000 in their account, and by the next morning it's at ZERO. **They got NOTHING for their $10,000 except for 6,500 fake clicks**.

And this is why Google is worth BILLIONS....

My personal business opinion. I don't care. **If cheating people out of their money like this is what I have to do to get rich, I'm passing.** I don't agree with it.

3. Turn your ads off at night. A lot of fakers are crawling around after 11pm.

B. Bulletin Boards & Forums (20%)

I answered questions on recording studio related bulletin boards and on forums, with my website in my signature.

There aren't that many related posts or questions for online studios daily, so I only visited these sites a few times a week.

Gear Slutz was by far the best site. I also used Future Producers, Home Recording Forum, and Harmony Central Forum. **The question answering site Quora was also very good.**

The posts are hit and miss. Sometimes a post will get hot and bring 100-200 people in a day to my website. A bad post will bring in zero...

C. Social Media (10%)

I never got into social media too much. I used to have a pretty big twitter account. I did some Facebook. I'm starting up my Youtube channel again in late 2019. We'll see how that goes.

I'm not saying social media doesn't work. I just never used it much, and this book focuses on *what I did* to make $100k a year.

D. Craigslist (10%)

This was great for one year! My first year, Craigslist accounted for 90% of my income. Mainly because there were only three online studios posting on there. Now it's probably over 1,000.

Year two, Craigslist put restrictions on postings making it very difficult to post in multiple cities. **I only used Craigslist for one year, before Google search results took over.**

Final Thoughts On Traffic Building

Traffic building takes time and diligence.

There *isn't* a free traffic source where you can spend one hour on it and tomorrow get 3,000 visitors a day to your website. I wish there was.

Now, you could have a viral post or make a viral video that gives you a huge traffic blast. *But that's luck.* You do get these once in a while, but you can't expect them daily.

Real traffic building requires getting your brand name out there in links and on social media, creating posts, making great content (articles and videos). This is what I did. **This is what ALL successful online companies that are primarily free traffic had to do.** But it's worth it.

And I'm not saying to quit your day job and implement these traffic building strategies full-time. Every day spend a few hours after work. It all adds up!

But if you never start, you'll never get anything going.

2. Great Results Are A Must!

Traffic is by far #1. #2,3 & 4 on my list could all be of equal importance.

I'm putting *Great Results* as #2 because if you're delivering amazing mixes and masters, **your repeat customers will be solid and your word of mouth referrals will be very good too.**

You want everything to be perfect, but you could still do very well long-term if you have decent traffic and deliver great results.

I've worked with over 7,500 clients. I would say 25%, *don't have a clue about anything*. Good or bad. You could rename the song they sent you for mastering and send it back to them, and they will say it sounds great! I've had this happen many times.

After a few days, the client downloads the files *he uploaded,* thinking they are the mastered files (even though they have the exact same name). Then he emails me saying I did an amazing job. **I'm like, "I didn't even start yet." Ha!**

25% *know a lot about music*, but will accept mediocrity because it sounds *better* than what they sent you, but not *great*. And they don't know what great sounds like. They might even ask you to make a revision that is absolutely wrong for their genre.

Note - This is how the auto-mastering software websites like LANDR get by. They deliver something that sounds **"better"** but it **does NOT sound the very best it can.**

If you just make a low volume mix +5dbs louder it sounds much "better." And it's impossible for any auto program to deliver exact consistency from song to song. This is another topic....

The final 50% of my clients, *they know their stuff!* They might send you an average mix that leans out of the genre (like a heavy bass rock song mix) but they know EXACTLY how the master is supposed to sound. **And if you're off, they will let you know.**

Most are nice about it if it's only one or two sonic qualities, like lower the bass and make the song louder. **But if you blow several genre specific qualities, they'll just ask for a refund.**   I learned this the first 6 months I was in business....

In this book, I'm not going to get into detail on *how* to deliver great results. This book covers the *business aspect* of building and running a successful online recording studio.

I go over this in great detail in my book, **Audio Mastering Secrets (186 pages).** In this book I tell you exactly step-by-step how I deliver great masters to my customers.

In my book, Song Mixing Secrets, I go over the top problems I see daily in client mixes, and how to fix them.

Get both books from Amazon and you'll have "Great Results" taken care of!

3. Creating A Solid Website

I'm going to list some elements I include on my website that I feel you should too. All of the elements were trial and error over the years. They were on and off of my website from time to time, so I know from customer response which ones are effective.

A. My CMS (content management system)

I use Joomla, but Wordpress is much more popular and a lot easier to learn.

B. Website Hosting

 http://BestMusicHosting.com (In Motion) has been my hosting company for all of my websites since 2009. **The best hosting company I've ever worked with. I'll never leave this company!**

C. Basic Layout

Keep the site simple, using only categories that you need. My recording studio website worked very well with the following categories.

About Us / About The Studio

This is an important page. I took it down for a while and noticed it negatively affected sales.

Potential clients want to know who they are going to be working with, who you've worked with, and how long you've been doing this? You can even put your gear list here.

Services/Prices

A lot of visitors want to see your prices *first*, and that's the *only* page they visit. **Make sure it's easy to find.** Put it in a couple different areas if you can.

Get Started

On this page, list step-by-step what a customer has to do to get a song mixed/mastered.

Before I had this page, I would get a couple emails *every day* asking, "What do I have to do to get my songs mastered?" **After putting this page up, I get a only a few of those emails *a year.***

Note – This page should also contain sub-cats like upload/download songs, payment, login, etc. These can vary and some websites don't allow customers to log in.

Payment methods I like are 2checkout and Paypal (a lot of clients prefer Paypal).

Free Demos

I recommend offering free demos, if you charge $20 or more per song. If you charge less, you'll get a lot of worthless trash mixes uploaded. Under $20, it's your call if you want to try it.

In the section "Working with customers" I talk more about free demos.

Note – **I do not offer free mixes.** I did it a few times and it was a big losing proposition.

Samples Of Your Work

I highly recommend before and after samples. When my traffic was at its peak, every day 1-2 people told me how much they liked my samples. Potential clients *do* listen to them, and if they are good they make a difference.

Most studio sites have a few or no samples at all. Having samples on your site gives you a big advantage.

Note – Make sure you have *great samples*, or at least good ones.

There are a few studio websites I visited that had *terrible* before and after samples posted. One guy's were horrendous! He had a couple masters up there that were very dull and obviously 3-4dbs lower than the rest of his samples. He didn't have a clue what he was doing. You would think *someone* would tell him to take the samples down. You'd rather have *no samples*, than some *ridiculously poor ones.*

Client Testimonials

This one is simple. List some of your best client testimonials. You can also list your best former clients here too.

A lot of future clients read this page. Sometimes they'll say, "I heard you're really good at.... whatever..." And they're quoting from my client testimonials. **They heard good things about me from *my* testimonials.** Proof that they work with some clients.

Blog/Tips
This satisfies Google's request for "great content" which they say helps boosts your website rank in the search engines.

Future clients will also find and visit your website from these inside pages. It's not all about just the home page any more. And the more inside pages you have, the more potential FREE visitors.

Contact Us / Email
Another obvious must. Potential clients have to be able to contact you. I use email only. No phone number.

I had a phone number on the website for many years and here's my conclusion. Note – This is *my personal experience* with a few hundred callers. **Yours may differ.**

Percentage-wise, not many clients call on the phone. Out of every *20* unique client emails I got it, I would get maybe *one* caller.

That came out to 10 callers a week, when my traffic was at its peak.

You're probably thinking 10 calls a week, that's nothing. Put the phone number up. But these calls did not go very well. Here's why.

Out of every 10 callers, I would get *one* paying job that averaged $90. If each call took only 5-10 minutes, it would be worth it. But they didn't.

It seemed like these guys just wanted someone to talk to. Calls lasted 30-60 min, and many times the same guy called back *several* times.

Most of these guys claimed they had 100 plus songs they needed mastered. Another reason why you're tempted to talk to them for days.

The end result - It was shocking that 90% of these guys never uploaded anything to my website! And the other 10%, it was usually one paid song, and a full CD maybe every couple months.

I then wondered if just having a phone number on the website affected *customer confidence*. Did a potential client see the phone number and feel the business was more legit? I would say, "**NO.**" A phone number on my website did nothing for me monetarily.

Proof - I *did not* have a phone number on my website for at least a year. I put it back up to answer this very question for myself.

Well, after three months with the phone number back on the website, I got *less* orders than I did the previous three months *without* the phone number.

Obviously, if I got *less orders* having a phone number up it didn't increase business.

I actually receive two emails a year where someone specifically tells me they only deal with websites that have a phone numbers. I give them my phone number and they never call. I don't get it.

Some businesses swear by phone interaction. Sales or consulting for over-priced stuff, a service people really don't need, or scammy propositions (like save 50% on your credit card debt), **talking to people on the phone is a must.** You have to talk them into something they would never do on their own. It didn't work for me.

Mobile Access
Once the website is done, it's a must to make sure it looks good on a cellphone. You want your website to automatically convert to a mobile site when needed, not show up real tiny on mobile devices.

Note – Google will penalize you in the mobile search results if your website isn't mobile friendly. They could even exclude your site entirely.

Last But Not Least
Make sure *everything* works for ALL devices. Do all the pages look right and are they linked properly? Does your MP3 sample player play on all devices? Make an order for $1 to see if your payment method works. Send yourself an email, and then reply to it. Does everything work properly? **Double check everything!**

4. Great Customer Service

I've worked with many small studios (as a customer) throughout my career. I've also worked with many various businesses. We all have.

What I'm going to write here is common sense, but it needs to be mentioned. Why? Because most of the small companies I work with don't do this!

Even if I'm dealing with the owner, many times he's a very lazy self-centered person. He doesn't realize (or just doesn't care) that this attitude causes problems. He will either lose potential jobs/orders, get refund requests, and he will guaranteed never get repeat customers with the way he runs his business.

Here's a list of what a lot of businesses need to be doing that I don't always see happening.

Get The Job Done Right

I've worked with way too many companies (people) who are totally consumed with their own time.

Doing what it takes to get the job done right **IS NOT** even a consideration for them.

If you want to have a great service, you have to do what it takes to deliver great results. And I'm not even talking about bending way over backwards. Too many business owners don't want to do anything!

Here's a non music related example. I have a music related example later in the book.

One of my ebooks, I used Fiverr to convert the word file. Four days after submission, the guy emails me a garbage file. It's converted, but text and titles are different sizes all over the ebook, and alignment is random. **The guy just ran it through an auto program and never even looked at it!**

I mentioned the problems and it was a fight. He wanted more money to do the job the right way. I said no, and he refunded my money.

Besides the obvious terrible job, the other problem is I just lost five days. Now I'm scrambling to find another ebook converter so I can make my deadline.

I see these poor rush jobs way too often. This not how you run a successful business.

Email Etiquette

I'm someone who really appreciates the hard work of others. And if they have a "success story" it fascinates me. If anyone does something positive, I'm the first one to congratulate them, and wish them the best in the future. That's just how I am.

That being said, I now realize most people are not like this...

It's important in businesses to *show* that you care. If you're not naturally like this, that's fine. **But the customer has to at least *think* you care, and are working in their best interest.**

How Not To Reply To An Email

I'll start this section with a little story. **It not only covers how not to reply to an email, but also details the rush job problem I just talked about.**

About 12 years prior to the release of this book, I was producing a band and needed someone to play some drum & guitar parts for five of the songs. I played the parts with sampler software and the musician played them live using real instruments.

There were several companies offering this type of service. I went with a guy (track musician) who had samples on his website that sounded great. Also, his prices were half that of the other companies (which doesn't always mean anything, I'm just pointing this out).

I was big into music production, song writing and arranging at the time, and was very proud of my CD. I later found many of my customers are the same.

I probably shouldn't have, but I wrote a paragraph for each of the five songs I was going to have him work on. The history of the song, the feeling of it, how he should play the instruments, etc. I also asked general questions, his prices, time frame, revisions, how to pay, etc.

So, the track musician gets this seven paragraph email, that took me over an hour to write it. He replies a few hours later later with, "See - Start A Project" on my website.

He *ignores my entire email.* Didn't even address me by name. **All he wrote was , "See - Start A Project" on the website, and closed with his name.**

I emailed him a second time with more questions, maybe two paragraphs this time.

He replied, "Yes, No, Maybe, No..."

After seeing how uninterested this guy was, my $1,000 job turned into $50. I sent him *one* guitar track sample and $50 to see what he would do with it.

When I got back the guitar track, it was a total rush job. It was just bad. I asked for my free revision and he fought with me about it, refusing to do it. I emailed him again and he never replied. He just refunded my money.

This is bad because people have deadlines. He put me a week behind schedule with this BS!

Six months later, his website was closed down. Out of business. Wonder why?

OK, there are two problems here.

1. With his initial emails, he will totally destroy the excitement of a client. I experienced this first hand. I didn't feel like working with someone who blatantly shows they have no time for me, or any interest in my project. His attitude made reduce the job from $1,000 to only $50.

Note – Yes, this guy was not very good and I was not going to work with him regardless. But, let's say he was great. Many potential clients will never even find out because they will never come back after his initial email, not even giving him a try.

2. Behavior like this shows he doesn't have time (for whatever reason) for his clients. He can't even write a few sentences and properly answer my questions? All he has time to write is "yes, no, maybe?" Then delivers a garbage rush job.

The client knows just by the email responses that he's not going to take the time needed to get the job done right and/or on time. **It happens way to often in all businesses, and many potential clients know this red flag.**

Many clients ask me, "Do you have time for my project?" It's important.

Note – If you wonder why *"I"* didn't see the red flag in my own example, this was all pretty new to me at the time. I now know what the deal is.

Give EVERY job the time needed so that it sounds the very best it can. Strive for excellence. You might not always be able to achieve it, but at least make it a goal.

Sound engineering is an art form. And if you don't take the time needed to get it right, you'll be delivering an inferior product that will get rejected.

And of course, one word replies are not very effective.

The Right Way To Reply To Emails

1. First and foremost, READ THEM to the end! I don't know how many times I send an email and get back a form reply that pertains to *only* the first sentence. And it doesn't answer any of my main questions.

2. Answer every question. And when possible, start with a direct answer "yes or no" and then an explanation or further details.

This is a clear way to answer, and the client doesn't have to figure out what you are trying to say.

Example -

If someone asks, "Can I have my songs in MP3?"

I DO NOT reply with *only*, "Yes."

I will write something like this, "Yes, I can send you MP3 files in addition to the .Wav files. Just let me know when the project is finished and I will send them to you.

This answers his question clearly and possible future questions.

3. I reply a sentence or two for each paragraph the client writes.

When possible, I read each paragraph and give each a couple replies that pertain to it.

And I uplift the project, the artist, their career. If someone writes they just finished their third CD, I reply with "How exciting! Congrats. I'm ready to help you make this one sound the best out of all of them!"

Don't miss an opportunity to uplift the client, and get them excited to hire you.

This business is more of a personal/social business than others. Unlike, for example, selling products on ebay, **you're working with someone's life passion.**

Some clients just like to talk music. If they do, go along with it. Treat your clients like a friend. It can only help your business in the long run.

4. Try to reply ASAP. At the very latest within a few hours. **When you do it's a powerful impression.**

If you reply to most of your client's emails within 15-30 minutes, HALF will reply, "That was fast," or, "Great customer service."

This is an easy first impression that clients appreciate. In a way it's the *opposite* of the one word guy. You're showing you care, and that the project is important to you.

The Closing Email

Ok, I only say these things if they're true.

I don't tell a client it was a pleasure working with them if they sent me 100 emails and complained about everything. **But if it went well, I will say it was great working with you.**

Note – But I still do always wish the complainer the best if luck!

I point out the positives in the project. If someone is a very good rapper or singer (and many are), they're a great song writer or musician, **I let them know.**

So many clients will reply with, "Thanks, no one has ever told me that." And I wasn't lying to them with my comments. **Many clients are very good in certain areas. Why not let them know about it?**

In closing, I thank them and wish them the best with their music, and let them know I'm here if they need anything else.

The Conclusion To - The Formula For
A Profitable Online Studio

Failing in business isn't *always* about not knowing what to do. The big problem I see with a lot of business owners is even though they know 100% what's required to be highly successful in their field of business, **they will accept failure rather than do what it takes.**

It could be a simple procedure that will take them from going out of business to decent profitability, but THEY WON'T DO IT!

Why is this?

1. Many have this mentality – **It's my business and I can do whatever I want, even if it means failure.** True! But why not do what it takes to succeed? Make "Do what I want" something that will make you money.

I've run several businesses with partners, and I've created website businesses for 50+ clients. **I've seen this behavior many times, but I can't completely wrap my head around why it happens?**

I get the, "Do what I want" attitude, but it's stupid. It's like the business owner has the right to fail, and he wants to exercise that right. **Just to say he did it his way.** Weird....

2. Or they're extremely lazy. I've worked with so many business owners (in many fields of business) who once I tell them their business idea will require 15-20 hours a week of free work (work they won't directly get paid for) to be successful, 90% of them either hang up on me or leave the room! Really! Or the conversation turns to silence, and I can hear crickets chirping. Ha!

They think a *service business* is a passive income business, where they have to do nothing but collect a fat check at the end of every month. Well, everyone in the world wants that! If it was so easy and no work was required, everyone would be doing it.

But what they don't realize is even with a successful passive income business it took the owner hundreds of free working hours, if not over 1,000, to create it.

If you want success, there's no getting around hard. Do what it takes to succeed and there's a good possibility you will.

Refuse to do what it takes and you will *guaranteed* fail. **Give yourself a chance to win!**

WORKING WITH CLIENTS

In this chapter, I'm going to give a few *must know* tips pertaining to working with clients.

How Much Should You Charge For Your Services?

As much as you can!

There are a lot of factors involved in the pricing of any service or product.

The two main ones for this business are -

1. What are your credentials? Who have you worked with?

2. How much traffic does your website get?

For mastering, I personally charged anywhere from $15 a song (when I first started) up to $50 a song. **Over the past several years, I've settled on $39 for one song.** For mixing I add in $3 per track/stem. These prices works for me.

$100 a song is the high-end for online mastering. You have some audio engineers with very good credentials who charge $50.

If you have no credentials, no before and after samples, and don't offer a free demo, you'd have a hard time getting $5 a song. Why would anyone give you money?

It's important to know that clients will compare your studio to those in a similar pricing range. They have a budget and will pick the best in that range, unless they find someone comparable that's a little cheaper. But *usually* they spend within their budget range.

And obviously, the less you charge the more potential clients there are. **But, that doesn't always mean cheaper gets the sale, as you will see in the story below.**

I once had a client who took me up on my free demo offer. He loved everything about my service, and said he would be back in a week.

Two weeks passed and I never heard from him. I emailed him and he told me he found someone else. I can't remember the exact price, but I was charging around $25/song at the time and my competitor was charging $40/song.

The guy told me he went with the $40/song studio because *since he charges more*, he's better than I am. But what about my free demo? He said it was great but I didn't charge enough, so I'm not that good. He told me this word-for-word. What can I say to that?

Just a little story to show you how people think. This logic is used in many service and retail businesses. Sometimes it's true, many times it's not.

Look at the competition and their credentials in your price range and set your pricing based on that. Then it's just trial and error, going up and down a bit until you find a price that works for you.

Should You Offer Free Demos?

The quick answer is "YES!" I offered free demos when I was making $100k a year, and I still do now.

There are a few pros and cons I experienced when offering free demos. **I will get into them after this story.** This story talks a little about the negative affects of not offering free demos, and we revisit not wanting to run your business in a proven profitable manner.

A few years *after* I created my online studio, I was talking to a friend in the business and he asked me to help *him* create an online studio similar to mine. He knew I was doing well and needed some help. He had the layout and text ready for me. It was decent. I created his site based on what he gave me.

He didn't have many credentials from past clients or much of anything else, so his site was very bare. I asked him if he had any before and after samples he wanted me to put up there, and did he want to offer free demos? He answered, "No and No."

Basically, all he was going with on his website was studio/gear pictures and the quote "10 years of experience" that he wanted on every page. I told him, "This isn't going to work. People want to hear what you've done, see who you've worked with, and hear how you are going to master their songs. They're not going to send you money just because they can see some studio gear pics, and you say you've been in the biz 10 years."

You can imagine his response.... "Just make my website how I want it! You said you were going to help me!"

At some point, making this website was stupid. **It won't work.** But he was right, I said I would make it for him, and I made it just like he asked me to.

His site was online. He paid for banners on my website and I sent a lot of traffic his way. And he got traffic from his own sources. **But after six months he called it quits and closed the website.**

While I was making around $9,000 a month with my online studio, we made about $500 the entire six months. And of course he blamed his woes on the Internet. **"The Internet sucks, man!"**

He's a good mastering engineer. He could have easily made $1,000 a month, and doubled that after a year. $80 a month was a joke.

Unfortunately, he was like the guy I mentioned earlier. **He exercised his right to do everything wrong....**

Now if you're a top engineer and you mastered Lady Gaga's best selling album, or Taylor Swift, Drake, Chance, Imagine Dragons, old school rockers like Kiss, Def Leppard, etc. you get the picture, **THEN you don't need samples or free demos.** Everyone into those genres knows your work.

BUT, if your top credits are the Polka booster band, a couple unknown rappers, and a half dozen rock bands no one has ever heard of, **you have to show people *something* that's real!** This is common sense, but some business owners don't do this.

Note - I have to mention one thing here. **I talk about free MASTERING demos.** I *never* give free **MIXING** demos anymore. I have before, but clients who want mixing are very picky, and mixing takes so long (hours per song). If I got half of my free mixing demo clients to commit I would still be losing money. It wasn't worth it for me.

The Follow Up Email

I customarily send a follow up email to customers who don't reply to the free demo. I would recommend doing this. A couple unique sentences to the project with a form letter. It sometimes positively influences the client, and doesn't take long.

Should You Send Two Free Demo Masters?

The idea here is if you give the client two different free demo masters to choose from, you double your chances of them liking one and picking you for the job.

I've seen only a couple online studios using this approach. One master they create is a typical radio standard master, and the other is louder and more open (lighter compression than standard).

So, should you use this approach?

Personally, I achieved great success sending only *one* free demo per person. But that's only because I first heard of this a couple years ago.

I'm one of those, "If it isn't broke, don't fix it" guys. I tried it a few times on larger project bids. I didn't notice that it gave me any advantage. The client told me which master they like better, then I was hired (or not) at the same rate as if they only got one free demo.

Logically it seems like a good approach and I wouldn't tell anyone not to do it. **Try it and see if it works for you.**

Any Tips On Beating The Competitions Demos?

When a client submits a song to you for a free demo, usually they submit the same song to at least 4-5 other companies. You're in competition with these other companies and the best master wins. Technically, it's the master that the *client* personally like best.

In this section I will give you some tips that help me beat the competition consistently, about 75% of the time.

I've worked on hundreds of re-master jobs. And some of these re-masters were done by some big studios charging $100+ a song! Not very often, but it has happens.

The client lets me hear what the other mastering studio gave them, and then I start with the raw songs and master the entire CD again.

These poor re-masters usually suffer in two areas.

A. Too loud/distorted, super bright, or both.

B. No compression at all. The song breaks up terribly when turned up loud.

1. If your masters are great in these two areas, right there you already beat half of the competition. Too many mastering companies fail miserably in these areas. Especially compression. They don't know how to use it at all. **I explain compression in great detail in my book, Audio Mastering Secrets.**

2. Speed is key. Within 12 hours, I would say 25% of the clients who submitted songs for free demos already chose which mastering studio they will use. At 24 hours, 50% are done. 48 hours, 70% are off the market.

If it takes you 3 days or more to get a free demo to a client, don't even offer them.

3. A little louder is perceived as better. Never send distorted songs, but if your demos are a little louder (+0.5dbs over industry standard) they will perform better vs the competition.

4. Once again, send a great initial email! If someone sends you five paragraphs about their career and their project, PLEASE don't *ignore the entire email* and reply, "Here's your free demo. Email me if you need me..."

Treat people the way you would like to be treated.

The Competitor Free Demo Test

When I first started out, I uploaded songs for a free demo on a few competitor's websites. I got back the free demos in 4-5 days, and the initial email was either one sentence or a form letter telling me how great they were. **NOTHING was said about my project.**

I asked one of the studios why the free demo took 5 days. He said, "It's free. What do you think, I'm going to drop all my paid client projects for your free demo?" I didn't reply to him. No need to. **He has the right to run his business however he wants.**

But the answer to his question is, "NO!" Don't drop your paid projects. Work longer and find a way to fit in the free demos too.

Me vs. a studio like this, my client already had his 12 song CD mastered before this guy even sends out the free demo!

Note – I want to keep the record straight here. During the peak of my online studio business, I was in the studio 12 hours a day, 7 days a week. Free demos went out within 3 hours, just like I preach in this book.

Now, I go into the studio every other day. This isn't the best way to do free demos, but it's not because I'm exercising my right to fail. I have two other businesses I'm working on at the moment.

What Types Of Songs Will Customers Submit?

You'll get all genres, but primarily rock and hiphop. How much you charge per song for mastering will determine the quality of what's submitted.

My buddy charges super cheap, $10-$15 per song. He told me half the songs he gets in are total garbage. Mono songs, songs recorded with a cellphone, big background noise, and horrendous singers. So bad, he stopped offering free demos.

I charge $40 a song, and $30 if you're a repeat customer. The songs I get in are high quality. Maybe 5% of the songs are poor. The rest are either good, or *very good* quality.

Are Some Potential Customers Better Than Others?

I'm glad you asked. **The answer is "YES!"**

Here's a list of potential **low sale** percentage customers.

1. Garbage mixes. First off, if you get a song mix in for a free demo that's total garbage, and your mastering brings the song up one level (from terrible to bad) 90% of the time the client won't even respond to the free demo after listening to it.

These free demos I either skip, or do a 5 minute one pass master on them. Usually I skip them.

2. If someone says they master their own stuff, **and they just want to *hear* how your free master will sound.** This is another 90% fail.

3. Artists or bands with a producer. The client will tell you they have a producer and *he* wants to master the CD, but the client wants *you* to master it.

Once he gets the demo back, the client tells you it's great, proceed with the entire CD. All is good. **A few days later the client emails you saying the producer finally listened to the CD and you suck.** Then it's a big fight for a refund.

This BS went on with probably 65% of the artist/producer combos I worked with. I hated even dealing with them. I would tell them before I even started, they're not getting their money back. The good news was this combo is rare. I saw it maybe once a month.

I get into this type of client once again later in the book.

4. The "Knock my socks off" guy. I also like the guy who says, "Ok, I submitted this mix to 20 different mastering companies. Whoever knocks my socks off with the free demo gets the job."

These are rare too, but I won't even do a free demo in this situation. Mathematically, you have a 1-20 (5%) chance of getting the job, and they rarely ever reply. This one's an obvious pass for me.

NOW, THE GOOD POTENTIAL CUSTOMERS!

One fact is that *overall* bands (other studios and labels) will pay more, and seem to be easier to deal with, when it comes to the money side of the business.

Solo artists, especially hip hop, are harder to get to commit to a project and pay.

This is because bands have 3-6 members and can split the damage. $90 bucks a man for a $450 mastering job is a lot cheaper than *one solo artist* coming up with the entire $450.

And when it comes to hip hop, *most* of the clients are young (18-23). Many don't have $450 laying around for pro mastering.

The upside is *if* you can get a hip hop client to commit to a project, many times they'll either have a lot of songs ready right off the bat, or they will put out consistent songs from month to month.

I *do not* recommend skipping over the hip hop demo submissions. You never know when you'll get a solid long time customer.

Here's a hip hop client story. One day I did six hip hop free demos. Not one person even replied to me.

The next day I had five hip hop songs in the que. I quickly did four songs, and then I got in a 15 song CD (paid job) and starting working on it. I finished the CD, and was ready to shut down.

Then I remembered I had that one free hip hop demo I didn't do. I was just going to delete the song. 10 hip hop free demos the last two days and I made *nothing*....

Then something said to me, "You already did 10 songs, why not just do the last one and be done with it?" So, I did it before shutting down.

The next day the last hip hop guy of the day (the one I wanted to delete) uploaded 20 songs and paid $680 in full! He loved the demo and said he had a lot of songs. And did he!

A month later he uploaded another 20. To make a long story short, over the next 2 years the guy upload 250 songs for about $8,000! **You never know who you are dealing with...**

Note – By the end of the month, a few more of the hip-hop demo guys in this story became steady clients. **What started out bad, ended up being one of the best group of guys I've ever worked with!**

Spotting And Working With The Tough Customer

I've talked to many studio owners who get totally frustrated by the tough customer. **In this section, I'm going to talk about how to spot and deal with them.**

I first must say, I don't get many bad customers. Most clients in this business are really great people.

Refund requests or scammy chargebacks, I get maybe 1 out of every 200 customers. Same goes for the rude obnoxious customer, roughly 1 out of every 200. They're rare, but when it happens they can really piss you off and create problems.

Note – Remember, I run my business very proficiently. If a business is run very poorly, every other customer might be a bad customer for them.

Out of 7,500 clients since 1999, I've had roughly 30-40 bad ones.

Here's what I noticed about them.

1. Too Many Emails
Ok, not every person who sends a lot of emails will be a bad customer. Most are not. But, 75% of my bad customers sent me an incredible amount of emails.

95% of my clients send me 1-4 emails per project. That's it. If I receive 25 emails for one project, this is odd and an obvious red flag.

One girl sent me 100 emails in three days for her 3 songs. REALLY! 100 EMAILS!

25 of the emails were a few paragraphs, the last 75 were only one sentence like, "Don't forget to make song #1 louder than the rest." And I got that same email four times.

I politely asked her if she could combine all her requests into one email. I told her I spent almost 4 hours on these emails (and I did, 2-5 minutes on each.) **She could care less... That's when she went crazy!**

She's telling me, "The customer is always right. I'm going to do what I want, don't tell me shit." I refunded her money and that got me another 100 emails.

Note – The customer is always right if *they* are the customer. If *you're* the customer at *their* job, you ain't right!

There's really no way to avoid someone like this. People like this are just evil. Who sends someone 200 emails, just for asking to combine the first 100 emails. And I failed to mention, the F word was in every sentence of the last 100 emails. Sometimes twice.

My advice is, don't add fuel to the fire. They could care less about you, so don't complain about what they are doing. They're doing it on purpose! You'll get no sympathy from them.

Try to end it and refund their money ASAP. Better yet, if someone sends you a bunch of crazy email requests, don't even take the job. I was new to this type of customer and waited four days before I decided to give the refund. **After four days, that puts the client behind schedule and they have another thing to complain about** (even though they created this problem).

The reason why these 25+ email people are many times a problem is because **they're either very demanding** like the previous example, but usually it's because **they're very picky and detailed.**

The vision for their project is VERY specific. And there's no way you could possibly know all of the details.

Here's a quick example of this. **I had one guy who sent me 50 emails for a song mix.** This was before he even uploaded his song tracks!

When he got the finished master of his mix, he rejected it in 4 minutes! From the time I sent it to him, 4 minutes later he emailed me. It took time to download the song and to write the email. **He listened to the song for under a minute!**

This is like the powers that be in the music industry. They listen to your demos for 10 seconds each, and they can tell you if your songs are hit or not. Yet 98% of the songs they release are absolute bombs! This is a topic for a different book.

Back to the mix story. His producer (very biased opinion) said it was terrible and he was going to mix it. I asked him what was wrong?

In the project, he gave me a bunch of little one word adlibs. He said, "The first adlib should come only out of the right speaker, then the next three out of the left. The fifth and sixth adlib should come out of the right speaker."

Ok, I'm supposed to know this? This is silly....

Watch out for these excessive emailers!

2. Bad Songs To Start With

If someone sends you grade "F" garbage stems or a mix you can improve only to grade "D" trash, **do you think anyone is going to pay you for that? They won't...**

When this scenario presents itself, I explain to the customer I can make this *better* but it won't be *great*.   If they're good with that, and pay, I proceed with no problems.

My rule is - I have to get all song up to *at least* a grade "C-" on a sonic quality level. If a "D" is the best I can do, I usually pass on the project or get a guaranteed money disclaimer first.

3. The Client Has A Producer

I mentioned this earlier in the book, but it's worth repeating because it's that bad.

It's one of the only scenarios where you will *in reality do a great job*, but be asked for a full refund a week or more later.

The reason why a problem arises here is very simple. The client is opting for mixing and/or mastering by an outside company. The producer does mixing and mastering himself as a business. HE wants the work! And the only way he can get it is if he tells the client your work is absolutely terrible. And many times he will...

Should I Ask Clients For A Reference Song?

I saw this question asked on music forums several times. And the answer is always, "Yes, of course. Then you know what the client is looking for." **This is a common sense answer anyone can give, *not based on actual real world experience.*** And it's a very wrong answer...

I've worked with over 7,500 clients since 1999. But, roughly only 200 clients either uploaded a reference track, or told me a band they're trying to sound like. Most of my clients just let me do my thing, without any recommendations.

I'm very good at matching reference songs. Well, a funny thing happened with these 200 clients. **An *astounding* 75% (150 of them) all told me word for word, "Wow, you did a great job matching my reference song, but I don't like it for my song!"** Ha! Then why did you send it to me and tell me to match it?

I really don't know why this happens, and there's no reason to elaborate. I've worked with enough people to know it's a fact. **75% of the time matching a client's reference track doesn't work.**

Armed with this information, if a client gives me a reference track or a band recommendation, I now give them back two masters. One is a reference match, and the other is how *I feel* it should be mastered.

What's the end result? 75% of the time they choose my master.

Just like in any other business, this is just another example of how *real world experience* trumps common sense and theory.

Using The Initial Preview As A Reference

Before I start mastering a CD project, the client gets an initial master preview of *one* song. They then give me any preference adjustments. Now I have a master they like, and I *could* make all the songs on the CD similar.

The question is, *should I*? The answer is, *yes* but loosely.

Most clients do well with the initial preview. If they approve it, they usually really do like it. It's rare for them to approve an initial preview, then complain about the entire project that you mastered similarly. This usually only happens if the mixes are very poor, which means the masters are too. If this is the case, you shouldn't have mastered the poor mixes to begin with.

Yes, I import the client's approved initial preview into the project so I can reference it for each song, but when the actual mastering process goes on, I **DO NOT** A/B compare it and try and replicate it *exactly* for every song on the CD. **I still try to replicate an industry standard song for every song in the project.**

I quickly reference the initial preview *only* to make sure all songs are fairly consistent. So all the songs on the CD form a "cohesive unit."

Sometimes the client's initial master does give you an overall preference you can use. For example, if a client says they want a warm, analog sound, and a little lower in volume, they will *immediately* reject a digital sounding loud master.   So, these preferences must be used on every song. But then again, this isn't exact matching the initial preview.   It's applying a few personal preferences you were given across the board.

Here's why I don't exact replicate the client's approved initial master preview:

1. Sometimes my initial master didn't use the best song mix on the CD. Even though the client approved the initial master and it sounds good, sometimes several other mixes on the CD are better, and will yield better mastering results.   **My goal is to make each song sound the very best it can.** I'm not doing that if I'm matching the entire CD to a master I created that used an inferior mix.

2. They might not have evaluated the initial master very well, and gave you bad preference adjustments.

This is rare (maybe 5% of the time), but it does happen. The client gives preference adjustments they don't entirely agree with.   If I made every song sound exactly like the initial master preview, they would reject everything.

3. All songs on a CD are slightly different. They have their own feeling and character. Sometimes the client throws in a few totally different songs. Many times you couldn't match the initial preview to every song even if you wanted too.

Go With The Client's Mix Or With What You Know?

Ok, I have to explain what I'm talking about here. **Many times a client submits a song and the mix is exaggerated in some area.** For example, a hip hop mix has *very heavy* bass, or a rock mix has *super bright* guitars.

So, do you incorporate these exaggerations into your master, or should you master the songs how you know they should sound for their genre?

Well, I used to think that since the bass was very loud or the guitars were very bright in the mix, that's what the client likes, so I'll leave it like that. **WRONG!** When I did that they would come back with, "What's wrong with you dude? These guitars are so bright they're burning my ears! Or, man that's way too much bass."

It's funny because if they "knew" there was way too much bass, why did they mix it that way and send it to me?

Master every song to industry standard. Now, you can lean *slightly* in the direction of the mix, but just a little. Client's don't want a master that's way sonically off, even though their mixes might be.

How To Handle A Very Poor Mix

Just so you know, if you're giving out free demos on your website and a very poor mix is submitted, you have about a 5% chance this demo will convert into a paying customer. Maybe even more like 2%. And if you send them a corrective action for the mix, maybe only 10% will respond. **When it comes to free mastering demos, I usually reject very poor mixes.** They're a waste of time for everyone.

As for paying clients who submit poor mixes, I email them back what the problem is and have them correct it. It's 50/50 if they can fix it or not. If they can't, they already paid so they'll get a free preview and we'll take it from there.

If a client approves a master that I know is not great and they want me to proceed with the entire CD project, I email them a disclaimer stating that all the masters will be similar and will not sound great. This is the time you should tell the client that 50% of the project price is a non-refundable labor fee, or you'll be working for nothing more times than not.

The Final Word

As you can see, there's a lot that goes into building a very profitable online studio.

I'm just one of many studios that have achieved this, but the way I achieved it is similar for all of us.

In this book I showed you what you have to do to build a successful online studio. Now you just have to do it!

I wish you the very best with your sound engineering career!

MY MAIN RESOURCES

Visit my online studio **JRmastering.com**

Check out my latest book. Available on Amazon.

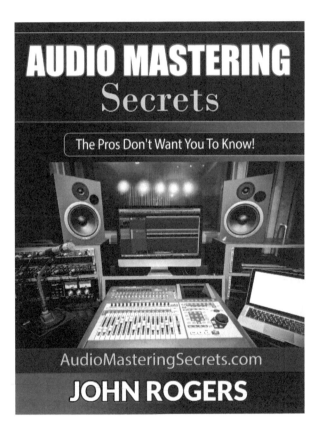

Watch the Video Series for Free on YouTube

YouTube.com/JRmastering

Also Available On Amazon.com

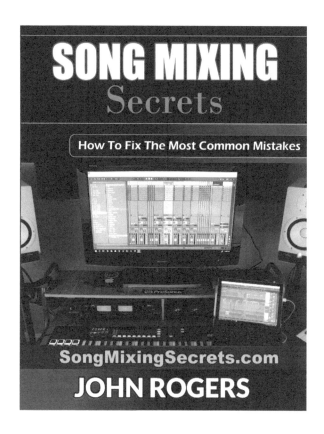

Thank You!

I would like to thank you for purchasing this book. I hope it will immensely help you start a successful online recording studio business, or improve your existing business.

Stay confident, work hard, and keep on learning. After 30 years in business and music, I still learn a little something here and there every week. **"Learning Is For a Lifetime!"**

I wish you the very best of luck in all that you do! Cheers! God Bless!

Your Friend,

John Rogers

Contact Info

Contact Me - info@JRmastering.com

Follow Me On Twitter - @JRmastering

Ordering Information:

Special discounts are available on quantity purchases by corporations, associations, and others. For details, contact John Rogers at info@JRmastering.com.

Made in United States
Troutdale, OR
12/06/2024

25927190R00040